Start Your Memoir Right

Strategies for an Effective Writing Launch

Denis Ledoux

Soleil Press

copyright © 2016 Denis Ledoux

All rights reserved. No part of this book may be used or reproduced in any manner whatsoever without the written permission, except in the case of brief quotations.

First Edition, First Printing
Printed in U.S.A.
Soleil Press

Book & Cover design: Sally Lunt

Publishers Cataloging in Publication Data
Start Your Memoir Right / Strategies for an Effective Writing Launch
— Denis Ledoux
1. Memoir writing. —2. Writing Craft. —3. Creativity.
I. Title.
ISBN: 978-0-9830931-7-6

For more information on how you can write a memoir—yours or someone else's, contact:
Denis Ledoux
The Memoir Network
95 Gould Road, Lisbon Falls, ME 04252
www.TheMemoirNetwork.com
memoirs@TheMemoirNetwork.com

For hundreds of stimulating and informative writing posts:
www.TheMemoirNetwork.com/memoir-blog

As a thank you for reading *Start Your Memoir Right / Strategies for an Effective Writing Launch*, please accept our gift of free ebooks, MP3s, and e-courses:
TheMemoirNetwork.com/Register

Soleil Press is the publishing arm of The Memoir Network.

Dedicated to all those
who dream of writing a memoir:
DO IT!

Start Your Memoir Right

Strategies for an Effective Writing Launch

DENIS LEDOUX

I.
Denis Ledoux won the 1989 Maine Fiction Award judged by Elizabeth Hardwick and the juried 1991 and 1996 Maine Individual Writing Fellowships.

II.
Over the years, we've been fortunate to have people speak well about The Memoir Network, about Memoir Network products and about Denis.

~ *Time* magazine wrote of Denis in an article on memoir writing in April 1999: "Since 1988, Denis Ledoux has helped thousands of people get started writing their memoir."

~ The *Christian Science Monitor* ran either roundups or feature articles on Denis. Three times.

~ His *Turning Memories Into Memoirs* was deemed by Booklist (American Library Association) as "very beneficial...helps writers get off to a great start."

~ Rhonda Kanning Anderson, co-founder of the early premier scrapbooking company, Creative Memories, said of his *Photo Scribe*: "*The Photo Scribe* has inspired me to a new level of photo-journaling. This practical step-by-stop guide can enable anyone to discover the depth of their memories."

~ *Bottomline Publications* acknowledged Denis's work (in a feature article) as a memoir ghostwriter, editor and coach.

~ *The Cincinnati Post* kindly praised *Turning Memories Into Memoirs / A Handbook for Writing Lifestories* as: "…a step-by-step manual, lots of examples, a fine appendix and a detailed index, making it a useful reference over time."

III.
Denis has also been interviewed on a variety of radio stations in cities as far flung as Boston, Philadelphia, Chicago, Los Angeles, Seattle, and Montréal. He has been interviewed by NPR affiliates as well as Radio Canada.

Table of Contents

Introduction: Laying the Foundation 13
Chapter 1: Are Your Reasons to Write
 Good Enough? 19
Chapter 2: Set Yourself Up to Succeed Later 27
Chapter 3: This is Likely To Be Your Most
 Difficult Challenge 33
Chapter 4: Lifestory, Memoir or
 Autobiography? 41
Chapter 5: Let Your Readers Show You
 How to Write 45
Chapter 6: What to Write Before You Write 53
Chapter 7: Launching the Writing Process 69
Chapter 8: To Succeed At Writing A Memoir,
 You Need Props 79
Epilog 87
Appendix: Bonus / A Journal Can Fuel
 Your Memoir Writing 89
Note from the Publisher 95
Gifts 95
Lifewriting Resources 96
Memoir Professional Resources 98

We hope you enjoy *Start Your Memoir Right / Strategies for an Effective Writing Launch* and feel, as we do, that it's a great tool to use as you assess whether you should write your memoir and plan how you should begin your writing journey.

A Word About
The Memoir Network Writing Series

The Memoir Network Writing Series will help you to write both more and more easily. In a number of short, laser-focused books—published both as hard-cover and electronic formats, you will access hands-on solutions to a number of writing challenges every writer faces—writers just like you and me.

We understand that you may have hesitations and insecurities about one aspect of writing and, when it comes to another aspect, you are confident and skilled. You are not looking for an encyclopedic overview of writing: you need a specific solution to a specific problem.

The Memoir Network Writing Series is all about just-in-time learning.

While we are specialists in memoir-writing, our coaching and editing has included a variety of other genres: fiction, how-to non-fiction, creative non-fiction, even poetry. The Memoir Network Writing Series can address the needs of many different sorts of writers.

Each of our books in The Memoir Network Writing Series provides easy-to-follow processes for optimizing the writing process.

To be alerted to publications as they become available, become a member of the free My Memoir Education. As a member, you receive many gifts, one of which is updates of publications via our newsletter, *The Lifewriter's Digest*.

Books in the series

1. *How to Go Beyond Writing Prompts / Answering Real Questions* (set for publication in November of 2016)

2. *Start Your Memoir Right / Strategies for an Effective Writing Launch* (Success—this book is in your hands!)

3. *Don't Let Writer's Block Stop You / How to Push Beyond Stuck*

4. *Write to the End / Eight Strategies to Thrive as a Writer*

Introduction:
Laying the Foundation

You know—or, at least, suspect—that it will take a lot of time and, ultimately, a lot of sacrifice to write what you so want to write. Writing a memoir, which is a full-length book after all, is not going to be easy.

But, it is not more difficult than you can tackle—if you approach the task right.

1) Are you ready?

Should you start writing now, should you wait until you are "ready"—and what does "ready" mean?—or, possibly, should you cross this project off your to-do list?

With these questions, your memoir-writing journey has already begun. That happened when you started thinking about writing. "Perhaps," you ruminated one day, "I might have something to say."

The idea of writing your story has perhaps fascinated you for a long time. So now you are exploring what actually writing the memoir you have been talking about for so long might be like. You may even have jotted down a few notes, and it has occurred to you—and this may have been a chilling moment but it need not have been—that writing a memoir is not the same thing as thinking and talking about writing a memoir.

Eureka!

Thinking and talking about writing is exciting, even exhilarating, but the actual writing might be full of tedium and discipline, of the dailiness of producing yet more text. It is not quite as exciting as speaking about writing a memoir. Not fair, but you can bridge the gap.

2) The shadow that falls between wanting to write and writing your book

"Between the idea and the reality, between the motion and the act, falls the shadow."
— TS Eliot
"The Hollow Men"

Between this excitement you are probably feeling about writing a memoir and the realization that it will likely require a whole lot of work falls the shadow of doubts and hesitations.

"But, ought I to write a memoir?" you ask again.

There are many reasons: writing a memoir will be transformative, and it will provide you with much satisfaction. That's partly why you should attempt it. (Another reason has to do with the audience that is awaiting your story, the audience that needs in some way to read your story.) But is there another avenue for you besides writing that can provide transformation? For instance, some people might choose therapy.

3) Your preliminary inquiries

There are many areas to consider before you undertake to

write or not write—so don't rush into it.

~ How do you think of yourself as a writer? You are more likely to persevere if you think of yourself as a "truth finder" rather than if you hold on to some romantic sense of being a WRITER.

~ Ought you to write an autobiography (a full life) or a memoir (a specific portion of a life)? Who will be interested in a full life? For most people who are not well known, a full life interests a family but is less likely to interest the public. Many of us have only a memoir in us. A single memoir may be all the public will want from us.

~ Do you need to supplement the information and the background you lack? Even if we are writing about ourselves, we have gaps in our knowledge of the times and of the players in our lifestories. Will you do this?

~ Have you enough writing supports (from computer to spouse) and, if not, how do you transform what you have into "enough?"

~ Can you mine your journal to bring depth to your memoir and more accuracy to your memories. (Memory is false, flattering, and feeble.)

The more thoughtful and prepared you are about what you are going to do as you begin, the more pleasant and rewarding the writing experience is likely to be.

The process of deciding to start to write has its own tasks that are appropriate for this time when you are resolving to initiate, or not initiate, the work of writing a memoir.

In composing *Start Your Memoir Right / Strategies for an Effective Writing Launch*, I did not set out to write a book about how to write the whole of your memoir. That is a bigger topic—one that I have covered thoroughly in *Turning Memories Into Memoirs / A Handbook for Writing Lifestories*. What I set out to do in these pages is to help you launch your writing effectively. (More help is available in subsequent titles in The Memoir Network Writing Series.)

4) A call for patience.

Inch by inch, it's a cinch; yard by yard, it's hard.

The lifewriting process will involve going through many stages. Each has its requirements and, generally speaking, when the requirements of a stage are not sufficiently met or not properly undertaken, the next stage is likely to be more challenging to accomplish—and possibly overwhelming. Be patient with the process: your success depends on it.

If you "lay the foundation" well, your writing will have a successful start and will likely come to a successful completion.

While the memoir project you are contemplating may seem to be a long and difficult one at times, it is not beyond your scope. The regular application of energy and thought cannot help but change you, center you, and bring you not only satisfaction but peace and contentment. And then…

One day, you too—as have so many people just like you—will have a memoir manuscript in hand.

I hope you can undertake to write your memoir. It is a rewarding experience.

Good luck and be in touch.

— Denis Ledoux
Lisbon Falls, Maine, USA
August 2016

Action Steps

1. Write about what is prompting you to write a memoir. Write about the following and more:

   ~ What do you anticipate your writing challenges to be?

   ~ Is the urge to write strong enough to see you through the challenges of the writing process? (Don't you wish people asked themselves this question about parenting before deciding to have children!)

   ~ Do you have something special to write about? Perhaps that is the experience itself or the perspective you brought to the experience or perhaps the conditions of the experience as they were sufficiently different to warrant being written about? In short, what is unique in what you have to write?

   ~ Is there an audience for this story? Who needs this story? Where do you have evidence that people are asking for the story? (Hint: look at what is being published as books and blog posts. If there is nothing on your topic, it is probably a sign there is little interest.)

2. Answer the "preliminary inquiries" in the #3 chapter section

of the above text.

3. Does the journaling you have just produced strengthen your resolve to write because it convinced you of the feasibility of the project or did it do the opposite?

4. If you continue not to be sure, is there another way you can meet the need that writing a memoir would address? Take seriously the Rilke quote that follows. If this book can convince you that you do not have what it might take to persevere and succeed at writing a memoir, then in this counsel not to undertake writing a memoir, you have received a huge gift of time and energy saved.

"In the deepest hour of the night, confess to yourself that you would die if you were forbidden to write. And look deep into your heart where it spreads its roots, for the answer, and ask yourself, 'Must I write?' "
—Rainer Maria Rilke, poet

Chapter 1
Some Good Reasons for Writing Your Memoir

Just as with so many big projects in life, you'll benefit by taking a moment to consider why you ought to be writing this memoir of yours that is intriguing you and what role you anticipate it will play in your life.

1) Telling your story in a memoir is satisfying—and sometimes therapeutic.

In late autumn of 1988, as people were hunkering down for another Maine winter, I was asked to read from my first collection of short stories (*What Became of Them*) to a meeting of volunteer Foster Grandparents.

My collection clearly made use of autobiography—the approach to fiction that has always compelled me the most. Several dozen men and women, sitting at long tables, many smiling in recognition of elements in the stories I had just shared, said in one way or another, "These are people just like us!" They seemed to recognize the child climbing the apple tree at the edge of the meadow or to glimpse once again their own parents in the tired women and men trudging through the tenement district on their way back from the textile factory.

After my short program of reading from my book of short stories, as has been my custom, I asked people to share their own stories with me and with each other. An astounding response—but, as I was to find over and over again, a completely natural one—occurred. In a torrent, members of the audience began to tell me their lifestories. These Foster Grandparents spoke with eagerness—as if speaking their stories were, at last, satisfying a hunger of long standing. Or, perhaps it was a need to preserve their story, to achieve some snippet of immortality if only in the telling to their fellow Foster Grandparents.

> *"Most of the basic material writers work with is acquired before they reach the age of fifteen."*
> —Willa Cather

Their memories were set in a number of countries around the world and in a variety of cultures within the US. As people spoke, some grew animated while others exuded peace. Some spoke with pride; others, with sorrow. All, however, seemed to need to tell the stories of their lives and of their families.

Once again, storytelling had "primed the pump" of memory to enable personal and family stories to pour out. After my reading that day, I left for home feeling justified in my faith in the primal function of storytelling to affirm and reaffirm meaning in our lives.

Like the Foster Grandparents, if you need to write—or tell—lifestories because you need to establish a "monument" to your experience in the "city park" of your memory—and of the world's memory—then you have a reason that may well see you to the end.

2) Stories need an audience to work their full magic.

I have also come to realize something more about writing, something that is a corollary of this need to be public: telling your story to yourself (in the privacy of your office, for instance) does not satisfy that hunger to tell. **People need to tell their stories to an audience.** Sometimes that audience is your own family or a few friends; sometimes that audience is much larger—as large as a city, a region, a whole country, or even the world.

Besides starting to write a memoir that records the story you so much want to tell, part of what you need to do (and I am going to guide you in doing this) is starting to address who the audience for your memoir will be. This can be considered in two ways:

~ who needs to hear your story?

~ whom do you need to share this story with?

Our ancestors told stories around the campfire. They did not tell stories just for themselves to themselves, sitting in the woods far from others: they told stories to an assembled group because they understood that telling and hearing were part of a process.

Yes, it can be intimidating to realize that your words are going to be read by an audience of real, live people—people who, in some cases, will criticize you. But, these real people—both those with appreciative remarks and those with cutting riposts—are part of your writing experience.

Don't let fear of audience stop you. In sharing your story, you will surely find an appreciative audience.

Action Steps

1. Write about why you want to write a memoir. You can get a bit philosophical here—and that is fine, even great. Compose a

lengthy response. A short answer will be insufficient. You can consider this to be your misson statement. Do you wish to:

~ Preserve a bit of history?

~ Set the record straight?

~ Celebrate your achievement(s)?

~ Show "the way" to other people?

~ Other?

2. Prioritize the above goals according to their importance to your drive to persevere and write to the end[1]. Which order of priority will most energize you?

3. The flip side of writing for an "other centered" reason is to write just for yourself. As you begin the process, while you keep others in mind, you can also give yourself permission to write without committing yourself to publishing your story. Most writers want some sort of publication (making public), but let it be ok for now just to write for yourself. Writing for a while without an audience in mind can be reassuring to the nervous writer. For most writers, a sense of audience will develop in time. The same is likely to be true for you. Your fear will abate, and your inherent joy in sharing will grow.

4. Place your writing from this Action Steps exercise—and all subsequent exercises—in a three-ring binder. (Print a copy if you have been writing on a computer.)

---

[1] See *Write to the End / Eight Strategies to Thrive as a Writer* in The Memoir Network bookstore.

3) You do have a memoir in you that is worth the time to write!

"Worth the time to write?" I repeated—raising my voice into a question—when a man said to me at a conference where I was speaking that most people didn't have a memoir that was worth their time to write.

"Not only is every life worth writing about," I countered, "but the writing of a memoir is a healing and developmental process for the writer. There is something in the telling of a lifestory that produces satisfaction and resolution and often growth."

"I don't know about the healing," he said, "but I do know that most people haven't done anything interesting enough to write about, let alone have someone else read it."

> *"Fill your paper with the breathings of your heart."*
> ~William Wordsworth

"For starters, I don't think children and grandchildren feel that way," I answered. "I've never met anyone who wasn't happy to have a memoir by a father or mother."

"Well, okay," he conceded, "but who else is interested?"

"First of all, the size of the audience is not what makes the writing of a memoir significant. There is worth in the telling itself." (I don't think he had read what I wrote in Section 1 above! LOL)

4) You want to share your story with another generation.

While there continues to be an insatiable hunger to know about one's family and culture, the man's commentary, of course, held an important point for you—for any of us—to consider. If you have not led a momentous life, are the stories you have to share worth the time to write them?—speak them, yes, because sharing a memoir is a meaningful way one generation transmits stories to another. But, writing them is so much more difficult—is the sacrifice of time and energy really worth it for you?

Let me repeat: *it is appropriate to write stories solely for a family or other small readership.* There is nothing "wrong" or not worthwhile with a small, familial audience. The value of any piece of writing is not measured by how many people—total numbers—have read it. This emphasis on size is a spin-off of the commercialization of worth. It is a result of the creation and promotion of the "superstar" in our culture.

The worth of a memoir is better measured by the inherent value to the writer and to its selected audience—whether that is your family or the world. The act of writing will change you and your relationship to your life. Writing is significant in itself.

But you persist, "Are there things a writer can do to create interest in a memoir if one wishes to write a book that goes beyond a small family readership?"

Yes, bear with me. I will help you with this, but the answer is for another chapter.

Action Steps

1. For whom do you want to write your stories? This is your audience. The answer could be as varied as: for my family; for parents of Down Syndrome children; for men who are about to retire; for

women who love judo. Describe the people you are writing for, their needs and their interests in some detail.

2. Why do you want to write for these people? In what way, do **you** need for them to hear your stories? In what way, do **they** need to hear your stories? Again, write lengthy responses.

3. Write about the immortality writing will bring you as your memoir and family history live on into future generations long after you are gone. Is this important and comforting to you—or not?

4. Keep you answers in your writing journal or place your writing from this exercise in a three-ring binder.

Chapter 2
Set Yourself Up to Succeed

Sometimes at the beginning of a workshop or of coaching, people ask whether there is a best way to begin. Well, of course, there is! That is the premise of this book.

The very best way to write a memoir begins with finding viable answers to your troublesome questions.

1) Writing a memoir is not going to be harder than you can do.

Writing any long piece requires discipline and hours of commitment to the task. You may have to learn skills you do not now possess. You may have to face a past you would rather not face. While your lifewriting may bring these hard moments to the fore, it is important not to dwell on these when they arise.

"There is no birth of consciousness without pain."
—C.G. Jung

As with parenting and all long-term projects, it is more constructive to focus on writing's pleasures and satisfactions than on its difficulties.

Many writers have felt that the benefits they derive from writing have made the effort of creating a memoir worthwhile.

You will find lifewriting brings you many rewards that will encourage you to continue writing.

2) Writing a memoir offers many benefits.

A. Writing a memoir can be like going to a reunion.

As you write your story, you will meet once again—if only on the page—many of the people who have been important to you in your life. Perhaps you will see your grandmother, smiling at you as she often did, about to tell you how pleased she is that you have stopped at her house on your way back from school, or your Uncle Edward's voice will boom in the background as you catch a glimpse your little sister zooming down a slide into a pool of water!

Commit to your writing, and your writing will commit to you.

Enjoy the vicarious visits! Everyone is still with you—if only in your memory.

B. Lifewriting can renew the relationship you have with your former, younger selves.

That, too, is a sort of reunion as you focus on the relationship you have, and have had, with yourself and your life. Perhaps you will want to hold the child you were and comfort him or her by saying, "You will be all right. See who you have become." Or, perhaps it is the adolescent you need to reassure. Or, all of these.

"Writing set healing in motion."
—Carolyn Roy-Bornstein
Crash: A Mother, a Son, and The Journey from Grief to Gratitude

Other writers enjoy the realization that they once were courageous or how noble in the face of adversity a younger self was.

C) Memoir writing is likely to be cathartic.

Over time, your memoir will also provide you with a catharsis, a healing of past resentments and pain. Too often, we hold on to the memory of a feeling long after the time when we actually still feel the way we once felt. That is, we confuse the way we remember we once felt with the way we now feel.

Memoir writing is not therapy but it offers you many of the same benefits.

And perhaps, too, the manuscript you are undertaking to write will reach out to others and speak to them about the life you have lived and the truth you have experienced. Your story can be more than an individual's tale: it can be the story of an Everyman or an Everywoman wandering through the past on the way to the present.

You are a hero who has adapted, survived, and perhaps even flourished in the world as we know it, and it is time to celebrate that.

> "We cannot become what we want to be by remaining what we are."
> —Max DePree
> Writer and businessman

Action Steps

1. Write about facing difficult memories. Do you have enough courage to face any unresolved difficulty you may encounter? (This inquiry into courage is not for everyone. Some people have resolved their difficult moments. While they may have experienced sorrow and loss, these are now in the past and are not weighted with pain. Do not feel you are remiss—or shallow, or unfeeling—if you do not have unresolved difficult memories to work through.)

2. Write about the emotional benefits you expect to derive from writing, from the process. In short, what you are writing about is what you hope to resolve.

3. If you expect there to be difficult memories, write about how you might deal with them as they arise. This exercise is more in the nature of a rehearsal rather than a prescription. Frankly, you probably don't know how you will react.)

4. What have your writing successes been? Congratulate yourself and let your successes encourage you if you should ever feel like giving up.

5. Do you keep a journal? Many people use their journals to explore meaning in their lives. Many writers have kept journals. Some, like Anaïs Nin, have made journal-writing their focus. Think of your journal as a laboratory. (See Appendix for a whole bonus chapter on journal writing.)

3) You can succeed at writing a memoir.

"Can I do it?" you ask, perhaps still unsure of yourself. "Can I write a book of lifestories that portrays my life's experience interestingly and accurately to family and friends—and perhaps even to people I don't know?"

Sure you can!

Writing a successful memoir may not be easy—I won't ever fool you—but you can do it.

"Any writer overwhelmingly honest about pleasing himself is almost sure to please others."
—Marianne Moore
Poet

Every year, people—perhaps just like you—decide to write one of their lifestories and, lo!, smitten with the bug of leaving a legacy, they continue story by story, until they succeed at writing what no one would shy away from calling a memoir.

You, too, can write your memoir and know the tantalizing success of achieving something you had never thought you would.

One woman from my Turning Memories Into Memoirs® Workshop, a woman with no prior writing experience, produced a book that was reviewed in Library Journal, a major American venue for pre-publication reviews. Hers was a sweet writing success that lead to speaking engagements, newspaper interviews, and, best of all, sharing her stories with an appreciative audience that was larger than any she had hoped to find among her own friends and acquaintances.

> "If we had to say what writing is, we would define it essentially as an act of courage."
> —Cynthia Ozick
> Writer

But, her real success—as yours will be—was achieving her once-elusive goal of writing a book to preserve the story of her life for posterity.

Success—whether you define it as private or public—can be yours, too, when you commit to the effort. You will have to put your "nose to the grindstone"—or more appropriately, your fingers to the computer keyboard—and work on a regular and, preferably, frequent basis. You will have to search for meaning in levels well beyond "who did what when" and you will have to pay attention to the mechanics of writing.

"But, I've never done this before," you might insist, sure that your situation is different from other writers in The Memoir Network and different from those of the hundreds of thousands of people across North America—and the world—who

> "Nothing is impossible. The word 'impossible' itself says 'I'm possible.'"
> —Audrey Hepburn

have already succeeded in crafting their personal and family stories into interesting and meaningful memoirs.

No problem! Neither had my writing student who was eventually reviewed in the Library Journal. She faced even a greater difficulty than most writers: not only had she, like you perhaps, never written before, but she had not spoken English, the language in which she composed her memoir, until she was well into her thirties!

Action Steps

1. Make a list of all things (and people) that will have a claim on your attention and co-opt your time and energy from writing your memoirs. In this list, include your lack of experience with writing and your little talent, your defective education, your sorry level of income, and any other excuses you want to dredge up from your pool of difficulties.

2. Go back to the list of items that you believe will block your success. For each item, find at least one way in which you will be able to make that problem work for you or a way to compensate for its shortfall (coming up with two ways is even better!)

For instance, "I'm too social to work a long time alone at writing." Ok. Here's how you can make that work for you: "I'll find a writing group to write with several times a week or, at least, to bounce my stories off."

3. Consider at least one way that you will make each of these supports (people or circumstances) even stronger. For instance, "My kids want me to succeed" can be enhanced by "I will ask if each of them if they can help me in specific ways."

Chapter 3
This is Likely To Be Your Most Difficult Challenge

Your initial—and most fundamental—challenge as you settle into writing your stories ought not to surprise you any longer, as it has been implicit in the previous chapters.

Your challenge will probably not be scheduling, nor discipline, nor writing itself—although these elements are not to be dismissed and will be discussed later in this book. Your stumbling block is likely to be something more fundamental.

Your most fundamental challenge is likely to be how you think about writing and about yourself as a writer! Without addressing this point in a positive way, without feeling good about yourself as a writer and about writing, you are not likely to have an easy time with your memoir.

Your sense of yourself as a writer is so important to your success, that I will devote a chapter now to going over some of the factors that may be holding you back.

1) You probably learned about literary writing in an inhospitable environment.

Let's go back to how you most likely developed your concept of yourself as a writer. Let's go to the time when you learned to think about writing, about what made good writing, and about what was worth writing about.

You probably learned to write in high-school English class which were usually taught by teachers who were not themselves writers. Of course, they knew about "good writing." Identifying "good writing" is what they themselves had studied in college, and they had become adept at describing it. They had been trained to be critics—not writers. But...

Somebody had to teach writing in your high school, and the best choice was the former English major who was your English literature teacher. The problem the former English major faced was that the process of writing, the process of how one goes about putting a text together and creating a polished manuscript—writing—is different from how one takes a finished piece—literature—apart and talks critically about it—critiquing.

Unfortunately, many—perhaps even most—high-school English teachers knew little about this process of writing a story. They had not been taught to write as a writer, nor had they devoted themselves to lengthy creative-writing apprenticeships. Their training was in logical writing—the essay—but how many of them had even attempted an essay longer than a term paper? And how many had embellished their prose with images and extended metaphors? How many had gone public with readings and publications?

So how could they teach you about being a writer of a two- or three-hundred page memoir that reached for style and clarity? A book that combines fact—but not logic particularly—with imagination—but not making things up. These men and women could teach you to be a literary critic as they themselves had learned to be, but how could they acquaint you with the process of taking an idea, a feeling, a memory, and transforming it, word by word, into a book-length manuscript? How could they teach you not only to feel comfortable undertaking to write a lengthy manuscript but also to be successful at bringing the writing to completion—by way of a story arc and sustained imagery and appropriate pacing?

> "A poem is never finished. It is only abandoned."
> —Paul Valéry

Obviously, without the apprenticeship, they couldn't. They had not done the work, never learned to be "writers." What they could do, however, what they were good at from having done a lot of it in college, was to critique your text—tell you what wasn't "right" about it.

As you heard what wasn't right about what you had painstakingly written, your confidence probably sank. You had done everything you could to make the text as "good" as it could be according to what your teachers had told you to do and now you were being told it wasn't good enough to meet the standards of the exalted writers they had studied. Perhaps you were simply not a good writer. (Well, there was a high probability you weren't, but isn't that why you were in writing class to begin with: to become a better writer?)

Another consequence of having teachers who were critics rather than writers was that you learned to over-esteem the editor role. This is not to say that the editor function is not important, but the emphasis may have unfortunately impressed upon you that getting stuck in the editor/critic mode was a virtue for which you should be praised. But...

Being stuck, remaining too long—or entering too early—in the editor/critic mode is not good for your writing. When you are mired in the editor/critic function, you write, you re-write and re-write so as to "get it perfect." The problem is that no one can ever get it perfect—no one.

> *"A man who writes well writes not as others write, but as he himself writes."*
> —Montesquieu

A better scenario would have been to have been trained to write much, write voluminously, and get your thoughts down, if not elegantly, then perhaps clearly. You needed to learn to trust your voice and your instinct. You needed not to be criticized but to be led by a sure hand, a confident sensibility, into literary creativity. You needed to be taught to collaborate with an editor rather than assume that role early in the writing process.

We must restate this: to be fair to those of our teachers who could not depart from this critique model, they themselves had been taught by former English majors who had been asked to teach writing without having the opportunity themselves to be trained as writers.

I'm not throwing stones here—I'm just trying to explain what seems to be the reality so many people—perhaps you—have lived.

Action Steps

This is an appropriate time to write about your writing history.

~ Who taught you to write and what were their "hang ups?"

~ What role has writing played in your life? Has writing been a joy or a burden? Are you comfortable with writing—with long writing such as you will have to undertake to produce a memoir?

~ Have you felt confident in your ability to create a manuscript?

2) "Excellent" models can be intimidating.

There was another daunting element about English class. Besides tearing your own "miserable" writing apart, your teachers had you read stellar literary works—novels, poetry, autobiographies—from what were probably called "The Masters" in your literature text. (Not that there's something inherently wrong with reading stellar writers—in fact, I encourage you to do so.) These paragons of literary style were famous literateurs whom everyone was said to admire even if few people read them outside of class.

Besides the literateurs whose writing was assigned, there were the memoirs that your teachers and texts alluded to, stories of famous and influential people. What you learned was that the only memoirs worth reading apparently were those of either powerful people who had played political or military roles or of famous writers—not of people like you and me. (Remember the skeptic in Chapter 1 who asked me if the memoir of an unknown was "worth the time to write?")

The course of history is obviously heavily shaped by powerful individuals, but it is also shaped by ordinary people who respond courageously and heroically (or servilely and cowardly) to the demands of their times. During the Vietnam War, antiwar protesters appealed to the common person when they wrote on signs, "What if they threw a war and no one came!" Eventually when enough ordinary people decided not "to come," powerful political individuals brought the war to an end.

There are many such instances of ordinary individuals whose actions have changed history. Think of Rosa Parks whose feet, one day, were too tired to walk away so that someone else could have her seat!

Remember: you do not have to have been an historical figure to write a memoir. There may be many ways in which your life encapsulates history.

Action Steps

1. You may not have been an important political or military figure, but you most certainly have done something that influenced the shape of history—even if not as big as Rosa Park's contribution, even if what you did was done by just you and a few others, even if the impact was felt only locally.

   ~ Were you active in the civil rights movement from a perspective that is little known?

   ~ Were you part of the turbulent sixties even if sociologists said people of your class or ethnicity were not?

2. For the next ten minutes, write a free flow of your memories of when you did something that was part of history. Do not worry about spelling, grammar or organization. No correcting, no rewriting—just writing. For ten minutes.

3. Is the story you wrote in #2 inspiring to you, motivating you? Is it enough to get you to write today, tomorrow, and the week after this? If not, which of your stories is? Linger with that story. It may contain an important element—prehaps the topic or the theme—that you ought to pay attention to.

4. Place the writing that results from this ten-minute exercise in your three-ring binder.

Congratulations!

By doing the "no re-writing" exercise in #2 of the above Action Steps, you have already begun to loosen yourself from the stifling grip of "good writing." You have begun to explore what it can mean to be a writer—and especially a writer of memoirs as you intend to be!

Remember: what you are about to do—write your lifestory or the story of someone else—is no different in kind than the memoirs prime ministers and famous actresses and insightful poets have written. Your memoir may be different in its impact on the world—and who even knows about that (did Anne Frank, an ordinary girl in a terrible situation, have any idea about what her journal would achieve?)—but it is not different in how it is written and put together.

Influential figures write worthwhile lifestories, and every year, meaningful memoirs are also written by ordinary people who decide to leave a legacy. People just like you—and me.

Chapter 4
Lifestory, Memoir, or Autobiography?

In this section, I am introducing you to a concept that is really something of a mind game—actually I've been hinting at what I am going to write for a while. If you still feel uncomfortable about writing your autobiography or memoir, this little mind game may just change your perception.

1) Stop thinking about writing an autobiography or a memoir.

Let the words *autobiography* and *memoir* slip away—if only for a while. Just for now, let these words describe what famous, important people write. Don't permit yourself to get caught in the paralyzing attitudes you may have from the terms *autobiography* and *memoir*!
Instead…

Write your *lifestories!*

Lifestories, memoirs and autobiography are, of course, the same thing: they are stories about you and the people in your life.

The term *autobiography* comes from three Greek words that mean "self" (auto), "life" (bios), and "to write" (graphein), and that is what you are now undertaking: self life writing. But, for the moment, give yourself a break and don't call what you are doing an *autobiography*. Call it a *lifestory*.

> "Writers, if they are worthy of that jealous designation, do not write for other writers. They write to give reality to their experience."
> —Archibald MacLeish

Memoir is a word derived from the Latin *memoria* which means *memory*. So a memoir is really an account of something you remember. It is what you are anticipating doing by acquiring *Start Your Memoir Right*, but again, for the moment, let the term be absent from your thoughts.

The term *lifestory*, especially in its plural form of *lifestories*, conjures the possibility that short narrations can transmit a full account of one's life.

Many people feel that the term *lifestory*, is more accessible because it is not weighted down with a long literary tradition, as is the term *autobiography*.

Lifestories, written singly just as they are told one by one, eventually add up to what is an autobiography or a memoir. When you envision your autobiography as a series of lifestories, the task of writing the stories of a lifetime becomes more accessible and ultimately more enjoyable.

This is another version of what I so often repeat: write your stories one at a time.

2) How is memoir different from lifestory or autobiography?

As we have seen, the term *lifestory* is simply a common phrase for either memoir or autobiography. But is there a difference between memoir and autobiography?

As the terms are used colloquially, there is no difference, but strictly speaking, an autobiography is about a whole life—birth to the present. Your kids will love your autobiography, the whole roll out of your days. The public may not. The public may appreciate a bit less of a roll out.

Generally speaking, an autobiography of a public person is more apt to interest a large audience than the autobiography of an unknown. That is why, when an unknown writes an autobiography, s/he often writes for family and friends. Most of us do not have an autobiography in us that will interest strangers.

Strictly defined, a memoir is about a specific period of a life: e.g., my memoir of abuse, my memoir of parenting an autistic child, my Vietnam-War memoir, etc. Because of the more narrow focus of a memoir, anyone interested in your topic—e.g., of parenting an autistic child—is likely to be interested in your story. A memoir (vs. autobiography) is about a short, more defined time or experience.

As a result, a memoir is often theme-driven, message rich. This message is often why someone reads a memoir—

to learn about how to live his/her life better, more effectively, more happily, to receive some guidance. While a famous person may have played a bigger role in history, an unknown—especially in that s/he is a "person just like us"—may actually prove to be more interesting due to the intimacy of the theme and message. While we may read with awe how a stellar figure handled an historic event, we are comforted and supported by the experience of someone just like us—e.g, we have learned a little bit more about being a parent to an autistic child and know that another parent has survived and perhaps thrived with much the same challenge.

Action Steps

In your journal or notebook, respond to the suggestion that you use the term *lifestory*.

1. Do you see any difference in the energy you feel around the terms *autobiography*, *memoir* and *lifestory*?

2. Does the thought of writing lifestories, one at a time, rather than an autobiography, free you? Does it seem easier? In what way?

3. How have your thoughts affected your energy and your ambitions for your writing?

4. Will you be writing an autobiography or a memoir? Why?

Chapter 5
Let Your Readers Show You How to Write

When I write "Let your readers show you how to write," I mean for you to imagine a reading audience, for you to visualize the people who will anticipate reading your story.

"But, I haven't written my story yet," you say in some defense of your lack of sense of audience. "How can I imagine readers?"

Simple: just ask yourself who would need to read your story. If you want to write about an abusive marriage, is it a big leap to imagine that someone currently in an abusive marriage or someone fresh out of one will be interested in your story? What does that person need to read? What will that person's questions be?

Let those readers whom, with some imagination, you can foresee awaiting your memoir inform the content of your writing.

Your sense of audience may—and likely will—change over time, but that is not a reason to remit exploring how you might meet your ideal—or natural—audience's needs and expectations.

You have already considered the possible composition of your audience in an Action Step. Now it is time to go deeper.

Whom are you writing for?

~ "I want to write for my kids and grandchildren. I want them to know who I was," one sort of writer will realize.

~ "It's important to me that my children and grandchildren know me, too," another will insist, "but I also want to place my life in a greater context. I'm hoping to have readers beyond my kin, readers who are interested in a larger picture of what life was then and of what I did. You might say that I am writing for a regional audience."

~ "I am not writing for my family at all. My experience has given me an insight into life and as a result, I believe I have something to share with the world. I want to get a message out. What I have to say is not geared to a regional audience. In fact, my audience may even be international. What distinguishes the people I want to write for is their interest in my topic, not their locale."

While each of these writers will create what we call a *memoir*, there will be differences in how the story is told and, consequently, in the sort of book that results.

The audience of family and friends is generally forgiving—the audience beyond it always less so.

~ The family audience is accepting of a memoir that adds up to a chronicle of events.

~ The public is generally not interested in a chronicle—and for good reason. The public wants a depth memoir. It also wants a polish in the style that a family audience will not find necessary.

Let's look at each of these possibilities.

1) A chronicle is worth undertaking—if you are writing a family-and-friends memoir.

A chronicle is writing that focuses on names, on dates, and on events. Chronicles do not interpret, do not seek a context larger than that of its characters. Family-focused lifewriters are more likely to write a chronicle because they wish only to tell the story of their lives as they have lived it. What were the summer days at their grandparents' summer camp in 1949 like—the cousins, the picnics, the sleeping late in the morning? What was it like to be in the 11th grade chemistry class? Something about Grandma or Grandpa. How many children did they have? How many homes did they live in?

These family writers are recording the facts of their lives for their children, their extended family, and possibly, a few friends. They are interested in who did what when. They are not particularly interested in the bigger picture of their existence—the opportunities and limitations afforded to someone born in their social, ethnic, religious group as compared to that of people in the larger society—nor are they interested in what sorts of deeper motives fired their actions and reactions.

Most would say "no!" to the concept of writing a hero's journey of their lives. And that's ok—for a family writer.

These people are what in the Middle Ages were called *chroniclers*. Chroniclers were not historians in the modern sense. Today, historians do their best to interpret events and look into the motivations of its players. Medieval chroniclers were satisfied with recording dates; they recalled names; they added numbers—but they did not look for causes or reasons beyond the most basic. ("The king was evil" or "God is good.")

If your goal is to be a modern-day chronicler for your family, that is already a worthy goal. I wish my grandparents had passed a chronicle of their lives on to me. By choosing to write a chronicle, you will also shorten the writing process. Your daughter-in-law who is "real good at English" and teaches at the local high school is just what your chronicle needs to proofread for spelling and commas and for a bit of tightening. (Of course, a professional can also be engaged for these services but that is probably overkill for what the writer has striven to create—a skeletal tale for a small group of indulgent readers.)

2) A chronicle vs a depth memoir

Start Your Memoir Right will certainly help you to write a better chronicle, but it is primarily intended to support the person who wants to write a *depth memoir*. A depth memoir—I've just invented the term so don't go to Wikipedia looking for a definition!—not only records the names, dates, and events but it searches for a larger view of the lives recorded. Such a memoir, just as the chronicle does, seeks to memorialize the summer cottage where the writer spent summers with his/her grandparents. But, it also does something different, something different that has to be defined as also "more."

What it does differently is that it explores relationships, possible causality, interactions. In our summer cottage story from above, the depth memoir would explore how, in those days, the writer's grandparents, who had both worked in a textile factory as operatives, were able to afford a cottage on the ocean. The memoirist (vs. the chronicler) will write something about the different relationship of income to land prices in that era or perhaps about how these grandparents owned the cottage with a number of other mill workers—each taking a time share. (I know of such a case in which the last surviving owner inherited the cottage, leaving third-generation descendants with an piece of ocean-front property that will comfortably subsidize their retirements.)

Perhaps these depth memoirists will also make use of this cottage story and other events and incidents to develop a theme of greater cooperation between individuals that was possible in another time in our collective history.

Because they want to interpret a time for their audience, depth memoirists include much psychology. They are interested in the hero's journey—theirs and those of the people in their story. These people want to write about larger issues and, to some extent, they succeed in writing the larger issues by including economics, politics, and psychology. While these are "off the radar screen" of the chronicler, the depth memoirist cannot imagine writing a story that does not explore the larger issues to the great benefit of the reading audience.

Eventually, if you are a depth memoirist, you will write a memoir that everyone in your natural audience will want to read. (Isn't it comforting to imagine that people are waiting for your memoir?)

3) A depth memoir is mandatory if you want to attract a larger audience.

Both the chronicle and the depth memoir are, of course,

worth writing. Who wouldn't want, as I have written earlier, to have a chronicle of their grandparents' lives? Oh my! that would be so special!

But, even more wonderful would be a depth memoir that would not only reveal to me what they did in 1948 but show me how they felt about events in their lives and how they apprised their roles in those events. I would also want to know what their regrets were and what they had wanted for their lives as well as when they did whatever they did. How did they cope with the limitations their economics imposed on their ambitions and how did it feel to learn a new language or a new way of life? In doing so, your memoir will become a story of Everyman and Everywoman—and not just the tale of a family.

How much of these things—the hero's journey—will your audience likely need to know? Keeping your audience in mind is a key to assessing the depth necessary to write a successful memoir.

4) A wrap-up definition

In summary, a chronicle is a lifestory that is not likely to appeal to an audience beyond family. Therein lies its limitation. If the grandma of the chronicle remains a total stranger, how much do we really want to know about what her beans tasted like? Interesting, of course, to some extent, but will this sort of chronicle carry a stranger—you or me or great-grandchildren— through 200 pages or, worse, 300?

The depth memoir, on the other hand, might also tell us about

Grandma's beans, just as the chronicle does, but the beans in a depth memoir would be part of a setting, of an action, of an historical era of a woman we have come to know. What the writer would really be telling us is not something about beans but something that is essentially Grandma, something about a woman of her generation, and about her personality and about Grandma's social class and about her goals in life and whether she chafed under them or not. Because this story would be character driven, the reader is more likely to want to read on—even if Grandma died before the reader was born, even if this grandma is not our grandma.

Have no doubt that the depth memoir—even of an unknown individual—can clearly appeal to a larger audience. The chronicle, on the other hand, is not likely to, and if by some chance it does, it can only do so to a limited extent. What a chronicle explores is too small, too circumscribed, to appeal to people who are not friends and family.

If you have been wanting to write a chronicle, even if your audience is family, I urge you—if you have the least inclination to do so—to transform your chronicle into a depth memoir.

If you start writing with a depth memoir in mind, you are more likely to finish with one.

Action Steps

Write about a memoir you have read recently and dissect what it was in the story you liked or did not like.

1. What was it about the story that held (or did not hold) your attention and kept you reading (or not)?

2. What elements in this memoir conformed to what I have written about depth memoir? (If you cannot remember a memoir well, get yourself one to read. Memoir writers should be memoir readers.)

3. What changes will you make to your projected memoir as a result of reading this chapter?

4. Commit to reading some historical, sociological or anthropological study of a period in your lifestory. Even if you are writing about a time and a topic you think you know well, explore your material more. For example, was your family typical of a family of your ethnic, regional or religious group—not just of the neighborhood or of your parents' siblings. You know about your family but do you know about families across your entire group (however you define "group"? This work is called pre-writing in the next chapter.

Chapter 6
What to Write Before You Write

Ok, you're getting closer to writing your memoir but you still have some prep work to do as you explore how to start to write your memoir.

What is pre-writing?

This chapter will help you succeed with the first stage of your writing. This first stage is called the pre-writing, the stage before you actually compose text.

Many writers are impatient at this stage. They are like the carpenter who is impatient to build and neglects to plan not only for the design of the building but neglects to order supplies and recruit help.

This chapter focuses on pre-writing tasks—tasks to undertake before you begin to write your memoir. That is why this phase of your lifewriting is called *memoir pre-writing*, and it is foundational to creating an excellent memoir. Pre-writing is often neglected or given short shrift. People will say, "I want to get on with the real writing!" But pre-writing cannot be shorted. It is a part of the real thing.

An important note: the tasks listed below not only occur before the writing happens (the "pre-" part) but pre-writing can also occur at several points in the lifewriting process: at the very start of the lifewriting task, as an effective daily warm-up, whenever you return to your writing after an absence, or whenever you feel "uninspired" to write (some people call "uninspired" "being blocked"—see *Don't Let Writer's Block Stop You*). Expect pre-writing to be often useful during the writing process—whenever you need the results pre-writing can provide. I'll keep calling this work "pre-writing" for simplicity's sake, no matter when it happens.

As a rule, it is more effective and efficient, not to start to write until you have done significant pre-writing. Pre-writing allows you to be:

~ immersed in the subject you want to write about so that you are "living" it, experiencing it in your imagination.

~ knowledgeable about the material so that you can write without the interruption of undertaking additional research.

Your memory—however you access it—can be false, flattering and faulty. As you start to write your story—or a particular part of the story, do your research and doubt every "fact" until you have proven it true.

Pre-writing can include:

~ list making.

~ perusing letters, journal entries, newspaper or magazine clippings.

~ gathering photos.

~ talking to people and reminiscing.

~ studying history texts—both in hard copy and digital.

~ reading memoirs and novels on the same period or topic.

~ doing some imaginative recreation of the past.

(I debated with myself about whether daily journaling during the writing process was a good pre-writing task, and in the end, decided to place the journal notes in an appendix as daily journal keeping did not seem specifically pre-writing. If you are interested in reading how journal keeping is important for a writer, go to the bonus chapter in the appendix. I'll let you decide if you want to journal regularly as a pre-writing task.)

1) List making.

An essential task as you launch your memoir writing is to create the Memory List. The Memory List is so important that it has its own book, The *Memoir Writing Plan 101*, in the Memoir Network e-book series. (If you have not added that book nor *Turning Memories Into Memoirs / A Handbook for Writing Lifestories* to your bookshelf, visit the bookstore at TheMemoirNetwork.com. See Chapter 2 in *Turning Memories Into Memoirs* for a treatment of the Memory List.)

A quick review of the Memory List.

The Extended Memory List consists of short notes (three to five words are sufficient) of people, events, relationships, thoughts, feelings, objects—anything—from your past. The list is usually random and always uncensored. Each line contains a different memory—and only one. When you write another memory, start a new line. Do not feel compelled to write in full sentences. In fact, I urge you *not* to write in full sentences! Write just long enough to recall the memory later. ("Hat" doesn't make it, but "Uncle George's brown tuque" does. In two months, will you remember that "hat" refers to Uncle George's brown tuque?" Probably not. I wouldn't.)

> *"Without memory, there is no culture. Without memory, there would be no civilization, no society, no future."*
> *—Elie Wiesel*

Your Memory List is always a work in progress because the more you remember and jot down on it, the more you'll remember and want to include. You will return to your list and rework it again and again as you write your lifestories. It is simply not something you do once and for all.

In addition to the Extended Memory List described here, there are also the Core Memory List, the Cluster Memory List and the Life Phases Memory List. Each of these has a role to play in the creation of your memoir. I do not want to repeat information here that is covered elsewhere in this Memoir Writing Series or in *Turning Memories Into Memoirs*.

2) Perusing letters, journal entries, newspaper clippings

Memory lists will help you to access much information and many feelings from your past, but there will remain many gaps. This is the time to look around your home and dig out the written artifacts you have kept (with any bit of luck you will have ample documentation.) These artifacts will help you to fill in the lacunae in your story.

You may, however, believe that you already know your story and that your Memory List is sufficient—after all, you are the one who has lived your life!

Most of us, however, don't really remember our stories—not even the ones we are so sure we remember well. What we "know" is a version that has evolved over the years as we "mis"-remember. There is a lot to be said for the theory that our memory is only of the last time we remembered an event or a person and not of the event itself nor the person himself or herself!

"I'll note you in my book of memory."
—Shakespeare

Those old enough to have lived through the assassination of John Kennedy often say—and certainly believe—that "you can never forget when you heard the news."

One fall, on the anniversary of Kennedy's death, I told my children about my experience of hearing the startling news. Later, in the process of writing about memory, I went back to my journal of that time. (I have kept a journal since I was 17.)

I was startled to learn that neither the "when" I remembered so clearly nor the "where" I was that I recalled in telling my story to my children were correct according to the journal entry—and I had written it at the time of the event!

It's a study in itself to ponder how we recreate ourselves and our self-images by subtly and unconsciously altering our memories over time. This is not malicious on our part. It may simply be because we do not remember the event itself but only remember the memories we have of remembering the event. So...

Don't assume your memory is reliable. Always crosscheck your Memory List "facts" with other people's or with written resources (your journals, old letters, newspaper clippings).

Action Steps

1. If you are a journal keeper, you can easily find evidence of the faulty memory syndrome:

~ Recall an incident that occurred at least ten years ago.

~ Write down the details as you remember them.

~ Crosscheck your memories by going back to the journal entry where you recorded the incident. Compare what you wrote then with what you've written now.

~ I am confident that you will find some, perhaps even many, discrepancies in the two versions.

2. If you are not a journal keeper:

~ Follow the above steps: 1) [recall an incident] and 2) [write details] to produce an account of an event.

~ Then cross check your memories by rereading old letters, newspaper clippings, diplomas, or other artifacts you may have. Verify the information by conducting an internet search. Be sure the sources are credible.

~ Ask others who were there what details they remember.

~ Now compare what you learned from your sleuthing on the internet with what you first wrote. Does new or different information suggest that you should revise your Memory List or written account?

3) Gathering photos

Your hard-copy and electronic albums and—alas, life being what it is—your unsorted piles of photos and chaotic computer photo files are excellent sources of information for your memoir.

The topic has been covered extensively in *The Photo Scribe / Writing the Stories Behind Your Photos*. Here briefly is what to watch out for:

> ~ The memories—facts and feelings—that spring to mind as you view the photos.
>
> ~ Details in both the foreground and background of the individuals (characters of your memoir), of the action (its plot) and of the setting. What do the details reveal? Everything in a memoir ought to focus on characterization. Who are these people—really? What cues do they give of themselves by what they are wearing and how they are positioned?
>
> ~ What photos are missing/were never taken/do you wish you had?
>
> ~ Prevalence in the photos of certain individuals, scenes and places over others.

The unbeatable benefit of photos is how they correct memory. You may remember clearly that Uncle Ralph and your mother were not speaking to each other in 1990 but there's a photo of them together in 1990 smiling—and not only together smiling but with arms around each other. Who's right—your memory years later or the photo taken on the very day in 1990?

4) Talking to people and reminiscing (aka: interviewing)

Interviews are basically guided conversations as you talk to people in person, over the phone or in an email. (Research is gathering information from sources other than people.)

Interviews will stimulate, supplement and correct your memory and will support and add to the facts and impressions you remember. They are also likely to force you to reconsider what is "true." (Of course, people are skilled at interpreting data in ways that meet their own needs. "Your grandmother always felt that I was right when..." "The Senator agreed with me that..." What comes out is geared to support the interviewee's position rather than Grandma's or the Senator's.)

In the best of situations, an interviewee remembers clearly and supports a memory with adequate cross-references, but as we have seen, time has ways of altering our memory. Interviewees  are themselves not immune from this problem. Sometimes interviewees may even forget (just as we all may) that, in the past they want to believe they know so well, they didn't even then know the facts. If it were possible to have asked them then, they would have admitted that they didn't know the details, but in the intervening years, the story and its details have been repeated so many times that they "remember it as if were yesterday!"

Often, what has happened is that they confuse other people's accounts with their own experience of an event.

It is also possible, because of the interviewees' young age or their needs at the time, that they had a partial or biased view what happened and why. A child, for instance, would not have much of a grasp of the sexual tension between his parents. A child would know that there was some sort of tension but would not know its source. (In short, it's possible some of your interviewees may never have had a grasp on what really happened—even if they believe they do.)

That is why our own memories and the memories of any interviewees have to be held as somewhat suspect until they are proven true. How to do so?

> ~ Written documents (see next section) are perhaps the most reliable source for retrieving data—the words don't change themselves on the page!—but written documents are not always available.

> ~ You may have to go to other interviewees for data that supports the information the first interviewee provided. In doing so, you may collect information that contradicts what your first interviewee said. You then need to find a third interviewee to pit the first two against. Who is right? Verification is not only a numbers game. The details have to be probable, based on the verified information you have gathered.

> ~ Alternately, you may have to turn to researching your topic.)

(For more detailed information on interviewing, go to *Turn-*

Action Steps

Prepare for an interview.

~ List the missing information you need to write your memoir.

~ Identify the people who might provide you with this information. Prioritize your list according to how knowledgeable each interviewee is likely to be about the information you need and how "interview-able" each of these persons is likely to prove to be.

~ Plan ahead. Set up interview times. Ask the interviewee to bring memory jogs: artifacts, documents, photos, etc.

~ Anticipate problems you are likely to encounter from the interviewee, from other people who may be present and from the location where you will be (noise, interference), and a schedule that will place its demands on your time and theirs.

~ In what ways could other people contribute to the success of this interview? Think of these people as props. (These persons may provide cues or suggestions to the interviewee: "I remember how your father resented that...") Identify who they are and ask permission to invite them.

ing Memories Into Memoirs, pages 89-97.)

5) Studying documents, newspapers, history texts—both hard copy and digital.

Look at diplomas, certificates, old letters and newspaper clippings.
Newspaper archives contain a plethora of information.
Besides the personal data, people always live in a social, eco-

From the Field

When I was writing my mother's memoir, she told me that my father had come home in the winter before their married—they married on September 4, 1944—and they had agreed that it was time to marry. (I loved it that he did not propose but that they came to an agreement they would marry. It tells me their understanding was solid, mutual.) She couldn't remember when he had come other than that it was in the winter before they married. When I asked her for details of where he was stationed and what he was doing there, she remembered that it was in the American South and that he was working on propellers, but not really where in the South nor what he was preparing for specifically.

I went to the internet archives of the newspaper of the city where my parents had lived and typed in *Albert Ledoux*—my father's name and *1944*. Soon—incredibly soon—I was reading an article about PFC Albert Ledoux on leave at his parents' house. The article mentioned where he had been stationed and where he would be stationed once he returned from leave.

This portion of my mother's memoir was now anchored in a reliable source.

nomic, and cultural context, and that context not only determined what happened to the people in your memoir but also interprets them for us now.

Perhaps you already know enough solid information about the period in which you or an ancestor lived to write about it convincingly and fully. It is more likely, however, that you have only a sketchy knowledge of the broad context of your story. Again, for instance, your awareness may be based on a child's limited perspective rather than the adult's broader, more insightful one. You may know what your family had by way of household items but not whether those items were commonplace in society at large or whether they reveal your family's special status (e.g., either more or less comfortable than society at large).

Even minimal historical research can help place your family story in a context that will round out your tale not only for yourself but for your reader by helping you interpret the actions and attitudes of your characters.

From the Field

Our memories can change historical facts about our own lives in order to protect us from some truth. For instance, I once heard a man in a radio interview explain why he had not gone to college. In the late '60s, he said, fewer people got to go to college than today because there was little financial aid available.

Since I graduated from college in 1969—which is late '60s by anyone's estimate, I knew, if ever there was a time when almost anyone who wanted to and had the grades to get in could go to college, it was the late '60s! There was an explosion in enrollments; universities in the U.S. were filled with first-generation students—I was one of them and I used the abundant resources available from new government-grant and -loan programs to finance the education neither my parents nor I could afford. The same was true of so many people I know.

Why did this man resort to an historical inaccuracy—one might rightly say "fabrication"—to explain his lack of education? The answer, of course, is complex and personal. It could be any number of reasons—shame about an inadequate education, covering pervasive hesitancy that might have characterized his life, not wanting to admit fear of the unknown or fear of bucking his family expectations, hiding his lack of ambition or academic ability. In his memory, however, the cause remained outside himself allowing his self-image as a "good guy who did everything he could but who was defeated by lack of resources 'in those days'" to remain unchallenged.

The challenge for the memoir writer is clear: memory can play a role in maintaining an unexamined life and/or self-justifying views. Therefore...

Every memoir requires historical research to justify, or verify, a memory.

6) Reading memoirs and novels on the same period or topic as yours.

Memoirs written by people who lived a life similar to yours or to your subject's can stimulate your memories and provide you with much information that can be used in your own writing. Ideas cannot be plagiarized; only words can. If you find material that you can use, express it in your own words. Do not plagiarize.

Reading memoirs dealing with your period or topic will jog your memory and expand your possibilities. Your story will be the better for it. Don't forget: the more you know, the more detailed the background of your writing will be and the fuller your stories.

About reading novels set in your time frame or your ethnic group or period: of course, you must distinguish between novels that were written by people who had lived the experience and those written by people outside the experience who are totally fabricating fiction. The latter may be in touch with the feelings of the novel but not with the details of dress and speech and housing. These are more likely to reflect the writer's own ethnic roots or the majority culture.

7) Do imaginative re-creations of the past.

There are two possibilities here.

A. The first is to envision an event that must figure into your memoir but which is now only skeletal.

Who was there? See the participants walk into the room and listen to what they have to say. Let yourself remember facts/data that had eluded you right before you began this re-creation. You will also begin to remember things you had no idea you ever knew—perhaps you did know once and perhaps you didn't. These "memories" are some you will have to cross check with your written sources or with people who were there. You will be surprised how many of your recreations are fairly accurate.

Some "memories," however, will not be. They may be influenced by novels you read, movies you viewed, or stories you heard and these memories will seem so real that you will swear they are attached to real life in the past.

As Reagan could have realized, while your visualizations are

> ## From the Field
>
> During his presidency, Ronald Reagan spoke of receiving a letter from a World War II fighter pilot who was shot down over the English Channel and survived to tell the tale. It was a stirring evocation of patriotism and of determination to vanquish.
>
> Unfortunately for Reagan (and perhaps fortunately for history), it was not difficult for radio reporters to find the scene in a search of Reagan's discography. The "memory of the letter" was based on a movie that Reagan had starred in some 40 years earlier! I do not believe he was consciously lying—perhaps he was then already suffering from the Alzheimer's he was to die from. Unfortunately, like many memoir writers, Reagan believed in stirring emotions and was never a stickler for facts. He also did not doubt his memory enough to do some cross checking.
>
> A word of warning—I know I've already said this several times already—always doubt your memories until you have proven them to be true.

likely to be true to your feelings, you must investigate to learn if they are true also to the facts.

Memoirs use facts to build their stories. Without facts, your memoir is a house of cards! It's a bad idea to believe your stories too easily!

B. A second exercise that will help you to access your past—especially how you felt at the time—consists of "make believe."

Re-create the story in a way you would like to have lived it. You will find that this exercise, taken from the world of therapy, will help you to access the energy of a relationship or an event. This "make believe" can be done as a drama in which you move around and speak (this is especially effective if there is an audience), as a visualization (with your eyes closed and everything occurring in your mind), or as a journal entry.

Chapter 7
Launching the Writing Process

Like all books in The Memoir Network Writing Series, *Start Your Memoir Right* is about a specific aspect of writing. It is about how to get you to start to write, about the process of evaluating if writing is something you ought to do and then how to go about launching the process. Now it has become time, at last, to look into the actual writing.

Do you have it in you to undertake writing a memoir and to succeed to the end?

What follows are tactics which, if you implement them, will launch you. Other books in the series, and certainly *Turning Memories Into Memoirs / A Handbook for Writing Lifestories*, can lead you through writing the core of your story. This book was not designed to do that. Its goal is to bring you to the threshold of writing a manuscript—and to do so elegantly and effectively.

"If there is a secret to writing, I haven't found it yet. All I know is you need to sit down, clear your mind, and hang in there."
—Mary McGrory, columnist

1) Allow first drafts to be first drafts.

Writing the first draft is really quite a bit different from subsequent drafts. Some people love first draft writing, while others hate it. Whatever your feelings about first drafts, know that there is no way around writing one.

The two drafts go together. Nothing can rightly be called a first unless there is a second. First grade implies second grade; first class implies second class; first book implies (why not!) second book; and a first draft implies a second draft.

A writer must expect to write a second draft, and a third even. No one can sit down and churn out countless pages of prose that won't need rewriting. Jack Kerouac claimed he didn't rewrite *On the Road*, but we know now that he was stretching the truth.

Writing a first draft is your opportunity to let all the words you have bottled up inside of you spill out onto the page. Your text can be as messy, as nasty, as melodramatic as you want or are willing to let it be. There are bound to be spelling errors, grammatical errors, factual errors, missing information, and overwriting. The important opportunity offered by a first draft is that of writing it all down. The editing function needs to be turned off as you write this draft—so enjoy the freedom.

First drafts are often meant to be a practice run. (Do you really think Herman Melville wrote, "Call me Ishmael" the first time out? He probably wrote, "My name is John." See what a second draft can do?) Writing a first draft is your opportunity to write wildly, feverishly, frantically. Use this opportunity well.

These thoughts on "first draft" are important because they provide you with a conceptual framework for the writing that will occupy the next months and even years. I hope that this section will lead you to decide:

> ~ "The first draft is a time to try anything and everything. Stick your neck out."

> ~ "The first draft is not the time to be a perfectionist and worry about style and polish too much. Let that come later."

Finishing writing a first draft is important because many of your anxieties about writing will vanish when it is done. You will know that you can, in fact, write things down. You will know that your stories will live on in some fashion, as unruly as that first draft might be. You will have a sense of accomplishment.

2) Disappointment follows the first draft

After finishing your first draft, you are almost certain to feel some disappointment with it—sometimes a lot of disappointment. You might even end up—I know this might make you gasp in horror—by chucking aside the entire first draft and starting from scratch again. This time, because of the writing you have already undertaken, your story will be clearer.

There can be no final draft without a first draft.

You'll remember the good writing, and happily leave out the dreadful prose, the heavy imagery, and the forced psychology. Or, you might take the first draft and a fistful of sharp pencils (or turn on your computer software editor function) and get to work pruning and primping. You'll look up the right spellings, correct the grammar, fill in the missing information, polish the prose, deepen the psychology

After the first draft, you will read your work with a more critical eye. You'll find places where you can expand your story and characters you can make more vivid—bring them to life. You will start to notice themes in your work and the way your story connects to something larger than yourself.

It is writing a first draft that has allowed you to get to the greater sophistication of the second draft.

3) Commit to write one story at a time.

Whether you are like some of my workshop attendees and coaching clients who want only to produce a few family stories or are like the people who always wanted to produce a polished memoir, you are likely to be daunted by the amount of writing you will have to produce to meet your goal.

Were I to tell beginning writers, "Your assignment is to produce a 300-page autobiography," most would blanch and then protest, "I can't possibly write that much!"

I tell them instead to "write one story at a time." This admonition is the antidote to the crisis of doubt you may feel at the beginning of your lifewriting venture. It is a workable response to "Where do I get off thinking I could ever compose a book-length manuscript?"

If this is you, don't dwell on the difficulties of a long autobiography; commit instead to writing lifestories that are just long enough to share at an evening gathering with family and friends.

When I ask new writers if they can write a three-, four-, five or even ten-page lifestory, most respond with, "Yes, I can do that." Over the weeks of workshopping (or tele-classing or coaching), I ask them to write ten, twenty, thirty or more such stories. Ten five-page stories add up to fifty pages while ten ten-page stories add up encouragingly to one hundred pages. Even better, twenty ten-page stories make a two-hundred-page lifestory manuscript! (Now, that's not too short to be a "real" memoir!)

In asking writers to write short segments of a memoir, I am on the one hand submitting to the brevity of time we have together. It is a serious constraint. But, beyond that, I also am teaching the concept of short pieces adding up to a coherent—and sometimes—lengthy whole. (I also hope to emphasize the process of storytelling, the pleasures of the writing process itself.)

"Inch by inch, it's a cinch; yard by yard, it's hard."

To ask yourself, from the start, to write a full-length autobiography would make the process intimidating. Just commit yourself to producing a number of short pieces. Won't undertaking a do-able—rather than discouraging—task encourage you to continue writing week after week?

That is my goal for you: to set you up to get off to a great start so that you finish your memoir.

The goal of the first stage of writing where you produce short pieces and even individual stories is quantity. The more stories you create in this first draft effort, the more stories you will have to polish and weave together in second- and third-draft work.

Action Steps

1. On top of each document page, write the name of your current writing topic as your title. (Your topic should come from your Memory List. See *Writing Memory Plan 101* in this Memoir Writing Series.)

2. Your memoir-writing goal at this stage will be to produce volume. Decide to ignore whether or not you are writing well or how your final draft will shape up, nor what the beginning scene of your story will be.

3. If you are ready to write one story based on an item on your Memory List, go ahead.

4) Don't worry how eventually the stories and vignettes can be pieced together.

When, in some future not within the purview of this book, you contemplate placing your stories together, there are two major ways this can be done. Knowing this now can help allay worries.

A. Some writers are satisfied with a manuscript that reads more like an anthology of separate stories.

Having written ten or thirty or fifty short pieces, some writers merely juxtapose them. Each story is independent of the one that preceded it and of the one that follows it. The only link is the chronology and emotional and thematic links that string them together. Often these books are called "memories" rather than "memoirs."

If this is you, then each finished, stand-alone story as it is completed is ready for your memoir and you can expect to have a book in short order.

B. Other writers want to weave their stories into a seamless whole—the memoir version of a novel.

They use transition stories and paragraphs. They link stories by creating sustained metaphors and images. They use suspense, foreshadowing, allusions, repetitions, flashbacks.

If this is you, you will organize later what you have written: shuffle the stories into a more appropriate order than they were written in; decide that the material on Page 4 belongs before that on Page 1 and that the piece about the picnic belongs after the piece about the conversation with your father. As you sequence your material, you may realize that you have already written something that can serve as a beginning or that you clearly don't have a good beginning yet.

I have often seen the first story written by a student/client appear on, say, pages 83 to 91 of the finished memoir and a piece written much later serve as the beginning of the story. This same thing may well happen for you, too.

Do not worry now about order as you write.

5) On any day—especially at the beginning, commence to write from anywhere in your story; don't feel you have to begin from where you left off.

In the workshops and in coaching, people often ask, "Where do I begin the memoir?"

This is a question you will have to address at some point but not now. Addressing this too soon can "freeze" your writing. At the beginning of the process, think only of what you will be writing on a given day. Let the memoir dictate where you will start writing when you sit at your computer. Write whatever comes to mind—without deciding how any of this will come together. At this stage, it is more important to write regularly and voluminously than to focus on writing well. Writing well is, of course, a goal, and it will come later

If on a given day, you know your topic but wonder how to approach it, your entry point can be a setting, a dialogue, or an action. Writing these will stimulate you. Paying attention to what you feel most compelled to write will prove to be not only the most enjoyable way to proceed but also the most effective.

6) Resist the urge to start writing from what currently seems like it ought to be the beginning of your story or be the next piece in the sequence.

On any day, simply start writing from the point that most commands your attention. This is the unconscious speaking to you. There is a coherence to its process—even if this coherence of the unconscious remains unknown to you for a long time.

One day, you may feel like writing about when you were fifteen. You sit down and you write the first draft of something that happened when you were a sophomore in high school. As you quit for the day, you are sure you will continue the next day to write about that time in your life, but the following day, when you show up at your desk, your interest has changed. You had a memory in the night about playing in a woods when you were six, and that morning when you prepare to write again, the memory is compelling. You sit down, and perhaps guiltily or reluctantly or perhaps eagerly, you abandon the half-finished story about when you were fifteen and quickly write the story about when you were six. This story about playing in the woods with your brother and sister is so insistent! Once you have written it and clicked "Save", you experience a great sense of satisfaction—or even perhaps relief.

Conversely, when you arrive the next day, you may continue

to write about when you were fifteen and continue to do so for the next two weeks.

Now, I'm not making a case for lack of discipline, for being flighty. It's just that when you are deeply moved to explore a story that moment is usually the best time to do so. The unconscious is primed to do its work. By allowing yourself to write in any order that comes to you, you are following an unconscious drive that is likely to lead to a rich store of writing—and meaning.

Be perfectly clear about one thing...

Your life—at least some aspect of it—is worth writing about. There is an audience for it, and you are the best person to write for that audience—one story at a time!

You can succeed if you commit yourself to success.

Action Steps

Write about what you have read in this chapter:

1. Once again: who is your audience?

~ Who will welcome your story and accept it as somehow theirs, as important to them?

~ Have your thoughts about audience changed any while you have been working with this book? How so and why?

2. Are you writing one story at time?

~ Does that feel like an opening or a limitation?

~ How have you adapted the advice to write one story at a time to your situation and is that working for you?

3. Do you want to write an anthology of stories or do you want a seamless autobiography?

~ Why is one or the other more attractive to you?

4. Do you have lingering doubts about your life being worth a memoir? Journal about that doubt.

~ What can you alter about your approach to writing to feel more confident about the process? For instance, are you writing for an audience that you are not comfortable with—does your reach seem too ambitious or not ambitious enough? Which audience would be a better fit? Are you afraid of your theme?

~ Journal about your fear, about the worst case outcome.

Chapter 8
To Succeed At Writing A Memoir, You Need Props

While the writing a memoir is all about writing, the actual composition of text, there remain many things you can do—like pre-writing—that not many people would actually call writing but which will enhance your chances of succeeding at writing a memoir.

In this chapter, I offer a potpourri of ideas to help you get started and to write more fluidly.

1) Write as a writer and not as a reader.

Remember the section in which I asked you to recall who taught you about writing? Most likely, as I had written, your mentor was a reader and not a writer, and s/he taught you to write as a reader not as a writer.

When you write as a writer, you come to a deeper understanding that the writing process is chaotic and messy and that it has many stages. A writer respects each of these stages and knows that launching the process of composing a memoir or other sort of book or as one takes up the writing for another day is important.

Where your story ought to begin for the reader—the point in the story arc or plot—is the subject of another book. For the moment, let's just say that your theme which will, of course, evolve throughout the process of writing will play a big role in informing you where your story ought to begin for the reader.

Action Steps

1. Look at a recent piece of writing.

   ~ Did you write the beginning of the story before you had written the rest of the story?

   ~ Did the beginning that was written before the rest of the story work for you? Would you change the point of entry into the story now? If yes, rewrite your point of entry (the beginning).

2. Take a story you have written and reread it in its entirety.

   ~ Note what the story is about. "About" refers to theme.

   ~ Is this reflected (even if only subtly) in the beginning paragraphs? What the story is about ought to be intimated in the opening page.

   ~ Re-write the opening paragraphs, if necessary, to reflect the theme of the piece.

2) Write in separate documents or on half-sheets of paper.

If you are writing in computer documents, label each document with the name of an item on your Memory List. Write as much as you want in the document. When you decide to move on, save and close the document. Later, you will cut and paste these different little documents into one larger document. That document will be either a chapter of your book or a separate story for your memoir "anthology."

If you prefer to write a first draft by hand (there are still people—good writers among them—who prefer to do first drafts by hand), filling a full sheet of paper with words is often the hardest part of writing—so take 8 1/2 by 11 sheets (I have often recycled paper by using the backs of printed sheets) and cut them in half. In the first draft, it is easier to fill a half sheet of paper with writing than to fill a full sheet!

On the top of each half page or document, write the name of your writing topic as your title. (Your topic should come from your Core Memory List or Energy Phases Memory List—see the e-book *Memoir Writing Plan 101*. It should already have clustered to it a number of other items from your Extended Memory List.)

Write whatever comes to mind on your short document or half pages—without deciding yet how any of it will come together. Remember: at this first-draft stage, it is more important to write regularly and voluminously than to write well (that will come later).

Remember: don't be concerned with whether or not you are writing well or how your final draft will shape up nor what the beginning scene of your story will be. Don't even worry about whether or not you are completely filling up a document or each half-page or whether some documents already read well or whether your half pages are full and others have only a few short sentences.

Once you have many documents, print them out. Then, take those pages or the stack of half-pages, shuffle them into an appropriate order: Perhaps page 4 belongs before page 1 and that piece about the bazaar belongs after the piece about your grandmother's cat. As you create an order to your stack of documents, you may realize that you already have written what can serve as an effective beginning or that you clearly lack a forceful beginning.

Not to worry!

In implementing this process, you will also discover clearly where you have gaps in your writing, where you need to fill in between what you have already written.

Keep writing.

3) Don't wait for inspiration to announce itself as a condition for you to write.

Writing is manual labor of the mind: a job, like laying pipe.
—John Gregory Dunne

Too many people put off writing, waiting instead for inspiration to do the hard work of writing their stories. When the spirit moves them, they sit down to write. And when the spirit doesn't move them, they say they have "writer's block."

This perpetuates the misconception that writers create only in some ethereal and rarefied sphere—not in everyday life. Inspired moments are wonderful when they happen—but they come infrequently and are absolutely undependable.

Since these moments may be few and far in between, waiting for them to make writing happen may limit considerably what you produce. Better to depend on discipline and craft.

For more on writer's block, see our e-book *Don't Let Writer's Block Stop You / How to Push Beyond Stuck.*

4) Learn to write in whatever time—long or short—you have available.

Because they lack big chunks of time, some people give up on writing altogether.

Ethan Canin, a novelist and short story writer, was a practicing doctor for many years. He would write in half-hour blocks when his schedule permitted. In this abbreviated way, day after day with some days allowing for periods longer than a half hour, he managed to produce an opus whose scope many writers would envy. Tillie Olsen, also a novelist and short-story writer, was a single mother who held a full-time job. She managed to write in short periods.

Action Steps

1. Schedule the hours of the day and the week during which you will write. Note these writing times on a calendar or date book and notify other members of your family about your commitment. If you get asked to do something during these writing times, think seriously about the effects of not honoring your commitment to lifewriting.

2. Can't the shopping or the movie or the visit be put off to another time rather than impinge on your writing? I hope you will learn to say, "I can't do that right then but I would be happy (if that's really the case!) to do that either earlier or later."

3. Set yourself a goal.

~ How many stories will you write in what amount of time?
~ Make the goal short term and not so big as: "I'll write my autobiography this year." Think of a smaller, more attainable goal: "I'll write one lifestory this week and every week for at least one month."

~ Renew your commitment once you have met your short-term goal.

Remember: underpromise and overdeliver. It works better than overpromise and underdeliver everytime!

4. If you find yourself procrastinating (which is what happens when you allow distractions), write in your writer's journal why you allow interruptions. What are you avoiding? What are interruptions really about?

5. Place your responses to this exercise in your three-ring binder.

5) Let your lifemate / housemate know about your commitment to lifewriting and ask for cooperation.

Does s/he know and accept how much time your writing will take? Does s/he respect your commitment to writing? Does s/he expect to do something with you during the times you are devoting to lifewriting? Do you need to negotiate about writing times? Make sure that you are not setting yourself up to be interrupted.

Negotiate with the other person(s). For instance, you can say, "If you leave the house every other morning so that I can write peacefully, I will leave the house to you when you want to have your friends over." Something like that, you get the idea!

A big sort of problem arises when your lifemate proposes "recreational" activities for times when you want to write. An example may be to go shopping for the new bathroom curtains in the middle of the morning because "there are fewer people in the store then." This may be true and reasonable but it also happens to be the time when you write the most easily. By going shopping for something you do not need now—the shower curtain you are replacing is still adequate although the color no longer "works" because the room has been repainted—you are trading writing on a project that is important to you in order to be nice to your mate (for whom your writing may not be important). Of course, there is nothing wrong to being "nice" to your  mate, but being nice in mid-morning cuts into your writing time. This will call for some forbearance on your part, to some holding firm on your resolution. This sort of conflict of needs is where many projects stumble in their march to success.

Of course, you can have this eviscerating conflict not only with your wife or husband but with parts of yourself—one part says "Don't be such a stick in the mud! Give yourself a break" while another part says, "But, Linda, you need to stay home to write."

6) Read memoirs.

I am astounded when I learn that someone who is writing a memoir is not reading memoirs. This is the equivalent of an athlete who does not observe other athletes play. A serious athlete is always looking for new techniques, for finesse of execution that s/he can replicate.

In the same way, a memoirist reads memoirs to learn how to write better memoir.

7) Workshops, tele-classes, or individual coaching can be useful as you learn your craft.

You feel like writing, write! You don't feel like writing, write!

Take writing classes—both for the benefits of working with a master teacher and for the support and examples of the serious and dedicated colleagues you will meet there.

Workshops and tele-classes can be local or national. They can last several hours at a time over many weeks or they can take place in a writing retreat for short, very intense periods.

A writing coach can also zero you in on the process and give you solutions to writing problems. Take an example from the visual arts: perspective. Winston Churchill, an avid amateur painter, spent two years teaching himself perspective before he realized he could have gone to a class and learn the technique in a matter of a few sessions and then move on to the painting he really wanted to do.

The same can be true of your writing. Some of the problems you are struggling to resolve may already have known solutions.

Epilog

So here you are: ready to undertake to write your memoir. *Start Your Memoir Right* does not contain all the answers you may need for your writing, but like all books in the The Memoir Network Writing Series, it does address a whole lot of them—enough to help you make an informed decision.

If you have read this far, you have probably decided to write your memoir!

What you are setting out to do—to write a book of your lifestories—is important work.

I have no doubt that you can succeed because many people just like you have already done so. They stood where you now stand—at the beginning of a journey that, at one point, might have seemed too long and too difficult—and they persevered and succeeded in reaching their destination.

You can succeed, too.

Good luck, write joyfully and be in touch if I can help.

Denis Ledoux
Lisbon Falls, Maine, USA

P.S. Once your memoir is published, send me a copy!

Appendix
A Journal Can Fuel Memoir Writing

Keeping a journal—regularly (even on a daily basis) can energize you and get you into the practice of both looking inwardly and of learning to articulate the inward understanding. Other forms of writing are more formal and their rules of writing may rob you of the energy to explore new forms of writing and feeling. Because of that, journaling can be an important developmental experience for you both as a person and as a writer. Because the journal is private by definition, you can write in it without fear of how others might react. No one will ever see it. Not ever—unless you want them to!

1. Keeping a journal can serve as a laboratory for your writing.

Scientists use a laboratory to conduct experiments. They check what results from adding this to that, from changing relationships and quantities and sequences. Sometimes when the results are interesting and prove worth pursuing, they continue conducting experiments in similar areas, pairing these findings with those from other experiments.

~ What have you noticed happens when you record your dreams? Do your dreams change? Do you change?

~ What if you make lists? Of people you know, of all the teachers you had in school, of sayings your grandfather had, of your mother's best traits. Has doing this given you any understanding of the subjects of your lists? Have you become more attentive to people and things?

~ What if you do free associations of ideas? What new idea have you come up with? Did any surprise you?

~ What if you recreate the past as you wish it had been? (You can even give yourself a commanding role!) Have everything turn out "the way it was supposed to! What happened when you did this?"

Let your imagination wander. You might just uncover long-lost dreams. This is your writing laboratory. Conduct the experiments you most want answers to.

2. You can also experiment with various styles and techniques to record your feelings and perceptions.

What if you write only in long sentences? Or, only in short ones? Or never use the word I? (Gadsby, a novel by Ernest Vincent Wright, is a 50,000-word book without a single e—except in the attribution of authorship!) Or use stream of consciousness (thoughts just as they come without any editing)? Where would this lead?

3. A journal can be a tool to get around writer's block.

Perhaps your writer's block—we can even call it beginner's block—is due to being cramped by the emotional limits you have imposed on yourself. Use your journal as a vehicle in which to break free to a more authentic you.

Keeping a journal can give you a place to experiment with your writing style, explore new themes and associations, and find your way around writer's block. (See *Don't Let Writer's Block Stop You*.)

4. A memoir-writing journal is spontaneous.

Journal writing is an effective practice for the memoir writer because it is a spontaneous and generally free-flowing activity. Because of that, it can be helpful to you in loosening up both your thinking and your writing style. Your journal is an opportunity to bypass the familiar rules that govern much of the other forms of writing—especially the essay form. In the journal, whatever you write and however you write is ok. You don't have to worry about form. For many writers—especially for new writers who are still caught in "the way it's supposed to be written," this is a great freedom!

Your journal is by definition, as most people would agree, a book that is not public, a manuscript that will only be read by you. Because of this, in your journal, you can safely explore the personal issue(s) that you may otherwise avoid facing—for fear of exposing yourself to public judgment.

How to best explore your issues in journals? There are many good books available for you to explore techniques for doing so. Read a few for their many suggestions.

5. What to place in your writing journal.

Here are a few suggestions:

> ~ describe events with as much emotion as you wish. Be blaming, accusing, melodramatic. Then assess how another person might have written about the events
>
> ~ write "letters" (that will not be sent) to people in your past to ask them to interpret their actions and words for you and then write their responses back to you.
>
> ~ rewrite the outcomes of past events so that you get the results you wished from them. Explore how it feels to have these outcomes rather than the actual ones.
>
> ~ recreate dialog the way you wish the dialog had transpired.
>
> ~ about your writing as has often been suggested in these pages.

These and the many more exercises you will find in other books will help you to come to an emotional comfort with difficult material that you may be—at worse—keeping from your memoir or—at best—writing in such circumspect ways so that neither you nor your reader are "getting it." If writing a memoir is to be healing, then the material needing healing needs to be explored.

Your journal is the place to explore these possibilities. As such, the journal is a pre-writing tool that will help you to start your memoir right.

A Note from the Publisher

A Simple Request

If this book contributes to your writing—whether to its quantity or its quality—would you please take a moment to write a short review of *Start Your Memoir Right* on your preferred retailer? Tell your fellow writers what they might expect of *Start Your Memoir Right*.

Thank You Gifts

We hope you have enjoyed this book. As a thank you for your attention, we would like to gift you with a free membership in the Memoir Network's My Memoir Education. Membership benefits include a ten-part introductory memoir writing course, and dozens of MP3s, including interviews with prize-winning memoirists to inspire and guide you. When you sign up for your free membership, you'll also receive the newsletter, *The Lifewriter's Digest*.

http://thememoirnetwork.com/members/

Lifewriting Resources
TheMemoirNetwork.com

The Memoir Network Memberships

1. My Memoir Education – TheMemoirNetwork.com/ Register

Benefit from a free membership in My Memoir Education / From the Inside Out. It is dynamic membership path for your writing journey.

Here's what we've got for you—FREE:
- A score of high-impact print and audio materials on crucial aspects of memoir writing.
- A dozen MP3s of interviews with prize-winning memoir writers to inspire and guide you.
- A ten-lesson introductory writing course to jumpstart your memoir with depth and fluency.
- An organized guide to the "best of the best" of the Memoir Network blog that all elegantly fits together.

2. The Memoir Network Forums – TheMemoirNetwork.com/memoir-forums

Consider the Memoir Café to be your online opportunity to receive complimentary coaching from The Memoir Network founder Denis Ledoux and your fellow participants. Membership in the free My Memoir Education required.

The Memoir Network Services

1. Coaching – TheMemoirNetwork.com/services/writing-coach

A writing coach will guide your writing project past difficulties and help you to bring your project to a successful completion. This service is effective for writers who experience blocks or lack focus or need technical help.

2. Editing – TheMemoirNetwork.com/services/memoir-editing

An editor will show you how to shape your story and keep your reader's interest while helping you to add finishing touches to polish your writing. This is especially useful for the writer who already has a manuscript.

3. Ghostwriting/Co-authoring – TheMemoirNetwork.com/services/hiring-a-memoir-ghostwriter

A ghostwriter provides technical skills and a writer's sensibility to your project as well as professional confidence, and you provide the details you want to share and preserve.

4. Book Production Service – TheMemoirNetwork.com/services/memoir-book-production

Start-to-finish pre-press preparation of your lifestory manuscript.

PLEASE VISIT
THEMEMOIRNETWORK.COM
FOR CURRENT PRICES AND SPECIALS

Memoir Professional Resources

Packages

1. Memoir Professional Package – TheMemoirNetwork. com/shop/memoir-professional-teachers-package/
A TURNKEY PROGRAM with a full line of supports—lifestory writing *Curriculum Manual*, how-to *Presenter's Manual*, *Editor's Manual / Editing Prose as A Professional*, *The Memoir Professional Speaker's Manual*, referrals from lifewriters in your area, and e-newsletter updates of your program schedule and services as well as a copy of the workshop text, *Turning Memories Into Memoirs*, and *The Lifewriter's Memory Binder*.

2. Associate Memoir Teacher Package – TheMemoirNetwork.com/shop/associate-memoir-teacher-package
Lifestory writing *Curriculum Manual*, how-to *Presenter's Manual*, a copy of the workshop text, *Turning Memories Into Memoirs*, and *The Lifewriter's Memory Binder*.

3. Editor's Start-up Package – TheMemoirNetwork.com /shop/editors-start-package
For the memoir professional who wants a strong start launching a practice as an editor of memoirs. Includes the step-by-step *Editor's Manual / Editing Prose as A Professional*, the entire Memoir Start-up Package, the e-book *Jumpstart Your Memoir Business Success*, and *The Memoir Professional Speaker's Manual*.

4. The Photo Scribe Teacher's Package – TheMemoirNetwork.com/shop/the-photo-scribe-teachers-package/
Everything you need to teach dynamic photo-journaling and

scrapbooking classes in a cost-effective resource package. The *Photo Scribe Teacher's Guide*, *The Photo Scribe Teaching Lesson Plans*, *The Photo Scribe / A Writing Guide* and *The Photo Scribe's Memory Binder*.

Individual Products (Package components)

1. ***The Editor's Manual / Editing Prose as A Professional*** – PDF – TheMemoirNetwork. com/shop/the-editors-manual/

2. ***The Memoir Professional's Speaker's Manual*** PDF – TheMemoirNetwork.com/shop/the-memoir-professionals-speakers-manual/

3. ***Jumpstart Your Memoir Business Success*** PDF
See *TheMemoirNetwork.com/memoir-professional-packages/* to receive this free e-book and a free subscription to the Memoir Professional newsletter and a ten part e-course.

VOLUME DISCOUNTS

Hardcopies of *Turning Memories Into Memoirs* and *The Photo Scribe* purchased in bulk are always available at a discount—both for The Memoir Network Memoir Professionals and others.

Web Affiliate Income Program – TheMemoirNetwork.com/affiliate-income

Don't leave money on the table! Earn money with every sale of The Memoir Network materials and services through your website. Visit The Memoir Network Web Affiliate Income Program for details and to apply.

Packages, Books, e-Books & Audios From the Memoir Network

PRICES ARE SUBJECT TO CHANGE. PLEASE VISIT THEMEMOIRNETWORK.COM/MEMOIR-SHOP FOR CURRENT PRICES AND SPECIALS

1. The Memoir Start-up Package – TheMemoirNetwork.com/shop/memoir-start-package

Turning Memories Into Memoirs, The Lifewriter's Memory Binder, MP3 of *Turning Memories Into Memoirs*, PLUS four e-books: *Memory List Question Book, Memoir Writing Maps, Start Your Memoir Right, Don't Let Writer's Block Stop You*, and 1/2-hour consultation with Denis Ledoux on how-to craft your memoir.

2. *Turning Memories Into Memoirs, A Handbook for Writing Lifestories* – TheMemoirNetwork.com/shop/turning-memories-into-memoirs

by Denis Ledoux
Hard copy & PDF

3. *The Lifewriter's Memory Binder* – **TheMemoirNetwork.com/shop/the-lifewriters-memory-handbook-ebook**
by Denis Ledoux - PDF Designed to fit a 3-ring binder

4. *The Consumer's Guide to Ghostwriting Services* – **TheMemoirNetwork.com shop/a-consumers-guide-to-ghostwriting-services-ebook**
by Denis Ledoux
Hard copy & PDF

5. *Memory List Question Book*
With My Memoir Education Membership – **TheMemoirNetwork.com/register**
Order separately on Smashwords.com www.smashwords.com/books/view/273427

6. *Memoir Writing Maps 101/ 4 Steps to Finding Your Way on Your Writing Journey* – **TheMemoirNetwork.com /shop/memoir-writing-maps-ebook**
by Denis Ledoux – PDF

7. *Start Your Memoir Right* – **TheMemoirNetwork.com/shop/should-i-write-my-memoir**
by Denis Ledoux – PDF

8. *Don't Let Writer's Block Stop You* – **TheMemoirNetwork.com/shop/dont-let-writers-block-stop-you-ebook/**
by Denis Ledoux – PDF

9. *How to Write to the End* – **TheMemoirNetwork.com/shop/write-to-the-end/**
by Denis Ledoux – PDF

10. The Photo Scribe Start-up Package – TheMemoir Network.com/shop/photo-scribe-start-package

The Photo Scribe, The Photo Scribe's Memory Binder, The Basics of Photoscribing MP3, PLUS A Cameo Narrative Writing e-book, *How to Add Stories to Your Photo Albums,* two Five Easy Steps exercise worksheets, *Writing Great Cameo Narratives* and *Writing Great Memory Lists.*

11. *The Photo Scribe: A Writing Guide / How to Write the Stories Behind Your Photographs* – TheMemoirNetwork.com/shop/the-photo-scribe/

by Denis Ledoux

Hard copy or PDF

A guide to turning ordinary photo albums, family scrapbooks and heritage albums into written treasures of family and personal history.

12. *The Photo Scribe's Memory Binder* – TheMemoir Network.com/shop/the-photo-scribes-memory-binder

by Denis Ledoux

Designed to fit a 3-ring binder – PDF

MP3s (Audios) From the Memoir Network

1. On the Road MP3 Package – TheMemoirNetwork.com/shop/best-buy-road-mp3-package
   by Denis Ledoux – 16 MP3 set

2. *Turning Memories Into Memoirs Audio* – TheMemoirNetwork.com/shop/turning-memories-memoirs-audio
   read by Denis Ledoux – 4 MP3 set

3. *Writing Basics: Getting It Right the First Time Around* – TheMemoirNetwork.com/shop/writing-basicsgetting-right-first-time-around
   by Denis Ledoux – 4 MP3 collection

4. *Making the Story Bigger, Second Draft Work* – TheMemoirNetwork.com/shop/making-story-bigger-second-draft-work-audio
   by Denis Ledoux – 4 MP3 collection

5. *A Miscellany of Writing Tips* – TheMemoirNetwork.com/shop/miscellany-writing-tips-audio
   by Denis Ledoux – 2 MP3 collection

6. *Getting Started: Launch Your Memoir* – TheMemoir Network. com/shop/getting-started
   by Denis Ledoux –MP3

7. *How to Publish Your Book* – TheMemoirNetwork.com/shop/memoir-book-production-audio/
   by Denis Ledoux – MP3

www.ingramcontent.com/pod-product-compliance
Lightning Source LLC
Chambersburg PA
CBHW020014050426
42450CB00005B/466